The Silent Project

Forged on the Anvil of Kashmir

Vidya Premkumar

Made with ❤ on the BookLeaf Publishing Platform
www.bookleafpub.in
www.bookleafpub.com

Dedication

Kunal, for teaching me how to break the silence
Shloka, for being the demanding mentor

Preface

The Genesis of Inspiration

The Silent Project: Crafted on the Anvil of Kashmir started as an idea when a poet friend sent me the June 11, 2024, issue of the *Outlook*, which featured 'The Silence of Kashmir'. As I read through article after article, enriched with excerpts from novels, poems, shayaris, and personal narratives, I was struck by the profound silence enveloping the truth of the situation. Each piece resonated deeply with me, prompting a need to reflect on these layers of silence —born from beauty and pain, political turmoil, and the enduring spirit of the people. I wanted to develop a creative project inspired by the silences I encountered in the issue and thus began this poetry collection. However, as an outsider, I felt the weight of guilt for usurping the voice of Kashmiris. To address this guilt, I chose Found Poetry as my medium, enabling my creativity to arise directly from the words and phrases of Kashmiri writers and journalists featured in that issue.

This anthology of 40 poems, split between free verse and Japanese short forms, is my attempt to distill and remix these narratives into a poetic dialogue.

Understanding Found Poetry

Found poetry is an art form where the poet takes book pages, newspaper articles, letters, or other existing texts and refashions them into poetry. Each poem in this collection originated from words and phrases culled directly from the magazine; these words were not just found but carefully chosen and reassembled to breathe new life into them, giving voice to the unspoken and often overlooked perspectives.

The Art of Remixing Text

Remixed poetry goes further by deliberately altering and reorganising found words to create something new and vibrant. This method involves a transformative process—maintaining the original essence while changing its form, like remolding clay into a new shape. The remixing allowed me to engage deeply with the text, challenging me to uphold its original integrity while imparting new meanings and reflections relevant to today's societal contexts.

A Political Work

This collection is undeniably political. It draws attention to the nuanced complexities of Kashmir's situation, using poetry as a medium to challenge, question, and empathize. The issues highlighted are multifaceted, reflecting the struggles and resilience of its people, the beauty of its land, and the often painful silence imposed by circumstances beyond control. Through this poetic exploration, I aim to ignite conversations, provoke thought, and encourage a deeper understanding of the realities the Kashmiri people face.

Personal Reflections

This book has been a deeply emotional and intellectually engaging journey. It tested my creativity and made me face uncomfortable truths through artistic expression. These poems provide a window into Kashmir's intricately woven carpet of human experiences, inviting readers to reflect, empathise, and connect with these narratives.

The Silent Project is more than a collection of poems; it invites you to witness, ponder, and respond to Kashmir's silent screams. As you turn these pages, I encourage you to listen closely—not just to what is said, but to what is left unsaid, for sometimes silence speaks louder.

Thank you for accompanying me on this journey. May these poems inspire your thoughts and awaken your senses to the profound stories forged on the anvil of Kashmir.

Vidya Premkumar

Acknowledgements

This book owes its existence to a circle of remarkable individuals whose support and inspiration have been my pillars of strength and creativity.

First and foremost, I must express my deepest gratitude to my partner, Kunal. He has taught me the value of being political and inspired me to stand by the truth and give voice to the silence. His unwavering support has been a beacon of courage and conviction in my writing journey.

Thanks to my mentor, Shloka Shankar, whose dedication and guidance have been instrumental in shaping my poetic voice. Shloka's rigorous editing skills, deep discussions, and passionate teaching of Found Poetry have honed my skills and opened doors to publishing opportunities I never imagined possible. Her exacting standards have significantly elevated the quality of my work, and I am eternally grateful.

To my mother, Usha Premkumar, who has passed on her creative genes to me. Thank you for encouraging my writing from the tender age of six. Your encouragement has been a constant source of inspiration, and I carry your creative spirit in every word I pen.

A special thanks to my son, Avadhoot Bhole, who has stood quietly by my side through our most challenging times. Your quiet strength and resilience have been a source of comfort and motivation, reminding me of the power of silent support.

I must also extend my gratitude to Nivedita Rao, whose keen eye for literary gems has enriched my world. Nivedita, the *Outlook* issue you sent sparked the creative journey that culminated in this book. Your thoughtfulness has been a gift that keeps on giving.

I extend my immense gratitude to the editorial team of *Outlook's* June 2024 issue for their attempt at telling the stories of Kashmir through the voices of Kashmiris, where the mainstream narratives have always been through the othering gaze.

Lastly, I acknowledge all the writers, novelists, poets, artists, and journalists who contributed to the special edition of *Outlook* magazine. Your poignant works on Kashmir have dismantled reality and revealed the dissent behind the silence, providing the foundational texts that shaped this book. Your words have not only informed these poems but have stirred the conscience of this collection.

I sincerely thank everyone who participated in this creative journey with me. This project would not have been possible without each of you.

I

oxymoron —
the tongue of Kashmir
silence

(Remixed from page 75)

II - Silence

Silence:

        it's subtle

        nothing but absences and holes,

    the shirts of the dead

        hollowed out,

  we'll all disappear

        as epitaph.

(Remixed poem from page 9)

III

still-born disquietude
the vertigo of a cold cave

(Remixed poem from page 68)

a soundless city
in the cuckoo's song –
the chained cypress

(Remixed poem from page 41)

IV - Game

The colonial game perfected
in the politics of democracy.

Neo-liberalism plunder
the mountains and trees.
Proxies and pawns
shift at whim.
Newspapers full of praise
of the 'normalcy'.
The election,
a mere performance.

Shift the yardsticks,
change the milestones,
prove desired outcomes
in record numbers.

The heaviness of silence
deeper in the theatre of the absurd,
Happy India.
Happier People.
From resistance to acquiescence.

(Remixed poem from page 33)

V

the shape of debris Philomela in Kashmir

(Remixed poem from page 66)

VI - Disappearance

6

The Indian moulding enterprise
thrives minute to minute in
returning Kashmir to 'normalcy'

which often means silence,
an open-air prison.

And the quiet streets are tonic immobility,
a politics of survival.

Where does resistance live?
in all hearts.

The phantom chambers of dissent
stand taller than the Ghantaghar.

(Remixed poem from page 32 of *Outlook,* June 11, 2024
issue, 'The Silence of Kashmir' special)

VII

Haer Parbat

new histories

on the skeletons

of the old ones

(Remixed poem from page 67)

VIII - A Makeover Project

A new style sheet is in place.
    "Ask no questions".
People are out in the street at night.
 Enjoy and don't talk.

This is strategic.
No watchdogs,
no human rights,
no politics,
discontinued poems,
working journalists have disappeared,
hip-hop artist no longer sings.

Silence is like a chewing gum.
 The day and night are stretched.
They are silent, we are silent.

(Remixed poem from page 11)

IX

skipping one parallel line for another Nouveau Kashmir

(Remixed from page 79)

after curfewed months
the self-censorship
of a thousand tongues

(Remixed poem from page 66)

X - Ghanta Ghar

the Ghanta Ghar
in the middle of Lal Chowk

      megalithic promise of resistance
hosted flags of freedom

the sentient tower
borne out of the worker class

      newly gentrified, loudly demarcated
now an ornamented spectacle for
      sitting, chilling and selfieing tourist

a behemoth of consumerism.

(Remixed from page 81)

XI

11

Naya Kashmir

rear-ended by a bus
while the policeman watches
another reel

(Remixed from page 82)

XII - The Festival of Democracy

The festival of democracy
has reached a crescendo.

People rise early
         and pray for the survival of Kashmir.

In the cold rainfall of silence
the theorist and the people you bump into on the road,

divert the conversation
to verse or two of Urdu poetry.

It is not the season
      of Faiz Ahmed Faiz
      but of Munir Niazi.

        They talk, but off the record.

The enveloping silence happened gradually.

(Remixed poem from page 21)

XIII

13

local bakery
the weight of small talk

(Remixed poem from page 70)

XIV - Manufacturing Consent

They make a desolation and call it peace.
-     Agha Shahid Ali

identity *Big Brother/ The Ministry of Truth/Thought Police*

measure   surveillance//   intimidate// altering//clampdown//coerce//manipulation//restricted// attack//propagating//raid//threat

impacted   statehood-homes-historical-records-press- individuals-versions-of-reality-autonomy-narratives- social-media-internet
-

manufacturing consent

(Remixed poem from page 29)

XV - 1984

15

doublethink

verbal directive
a 53-page media policy
crackdown on narrative builders

thoughtcrime

somehow,
the persistent wildflowers
defy the silence

(Remixed poem from page 30)

XVI - Policed

16

Policed
the length and breadth of Kashmir.

Even a sigh
if not jailed,
is measured
and recorded for censorship.

New ways in which
the bodies, homes, streets, waters and skies
do not matter.

(Remixed poem from page 31)

XVII

17

high-risk words the dictatorship of silence

(Remixed poem from page 67)

XVIII - When Truth is a Lie

Social media find
malleable and agreeable voices within.

Arsenal of concocted, planted and false narrative
and information blockade
systematically implements manufactured silence.

Dissent and disagreement
exist in isolation and alienation,
disillusioned.
Truth replaced by silence is a lie.

(Remixed poem from page 37)

XIX

the scent of barbed wire *gul toor*

(Remixed from page 75)
Gul toor is Kashmiri name for Yellow Amaryllis.

a permanent noose–
the witch-hunt of the family
of the dissenter

(Remixed poem from page 38)

XX - Ordinary Things

Ordinary things disappear.
Disappearances are continual.

     And yet,
people fill their days with metaphors,
the personal archives of birds, flowers, photographs,
calendars, maps and diaries.

     Living here is an ordeal.
     The passport to memory   is under review.
Everyday, when the people wake up
     something ordinary disappears.

(Remixed poem from page 10)

XXI

21

an unfinished meal
of chai and tchot
in the fleeing trucks
hands smeared with dough
embrace the cylinder

(Remixed poem from page 45)

XXII - Disappearances

DISAPPEARANCES ARE NORMAL.

8000 people disappeared.
Nobody knows where to
look for them.

discredited,
dismissed,
dismembered,

faded
are the stories of silence.

Conspiracy theories in this silence.
A forever siege of words.
What if words finally disappeared
while the bell rings in new hour in the Ghanta Ghar at
Lal Chowk.

(Remixed poem from page 17)

XXIII

wooden chest
full of heirloom memories –
my domicile certificate

(Remixed poem from page 46)

a wish between
real and imagined home –
passage of a comet

(Remixed poem from page 46)

XXIV - A Strange Lull

24

a ramshackle hope fading,
I am watching
wish knots never untied,

wishes never granted.

Trapped in the burden of legacy,
I just watch everything.
There will be a proper time
to tell each other stories,
for art to express fears and hopes and losses.

I am waiting in silence.
Silence is not peace.
Nothing is normal in silence.

(Remixed poem from page 14)

XXV

       manifest legacy of silence *haalat*

(Remixed from page 75)

the withered tulips
in May storms
unshed bullets
draft into
old sorrows

(Remixed poem from page 72)

XXVI - The Story of Silence

Is the story of silence

           a story of anonymity?

Where is the record of silence
when nobody speaks?
Isn't it poems for the dead?

           The silence in the peace
               is a volcano.

We don't know what our sadness is,
for a lot of newness and transition
takes time

        to absorb.

           But the documents of silence
             will be written
            when the original cause
             of imposed silence
             offends the people.

(Remixed poem from page 12)

XXVII

winter wilderness –
the comatose belly
of oblivion

(Remixed poem from page 68)

XXVIII - Positivity

persuasive silence
can explode into something unexpected.

shut one's eyes,
focus on the good things,
move on.
tsunami of positive thinking.

road is bad	good road elsewhere
power cuts	restoration of power
lack of facilities	facilities that exist

Enjoy Switzerland while in Kashmir.

Collective decision,
remain silent to those outside the circle
These days silence is better.

(Remixed poem from page 22)

XXIX

snow dunes
  who has ever undone
  a burial?

(Remixed poem from page 68)

XXX - The Long Silence

Tchpe chai rupsanzi, kar kha tai son sanzi
(Silence is silver. If you maintain it, it is gold.)

This long silence
was an act of self-preservation,
was an act of self-defence.

There is peace at an emotional cost.
Have no expectations,
Sadness all over.
We are not talking to each other.

This long cycle of silence
needs articulation.
Things might change from
talking and breaking the silence.

To articulate is a provocation.
There is a cost to talking.
But once the conversations begin,
We reclaim our voice.
We create space
to end the existing suffocation.,
Give hope,

help people heal.

(Remixed poem from page 35)

XXXI

32

hope of rebuilding
their homeland in Kashmir –

voting in Jammu

(Remixed poem from page 46)

XXXII - The Pear

The pear grew just out of reach

decided to end the tyranny of the pear

mapped
the next manoeuvre

heave off the ground
foot at the Y of two branches
pull up (scraping the flesh)
scan the garden
lean towards the pear
precarious balancing act
push on regardless
sinews stretched to the limits
finally
tug the pear free from bondage
bite into its gentle sweetness
savouring its soft flesh.

Exuberance lingers around and holds court.

(Remixed from page 71)

33

XXXIII

34

at sunset
the silhouette of the birds
my parents' winter stories

(Remixed from page 74)

XXXIV - Poetry

35

when between memories and apples
words get hunted into extinction,
the silence of an empty Jamia Masjid
devours all conversations,
the only recourse is poetry,
poetry will be the envoy bearing
good tidings in a promised dawn.

(Remixed from page 73)

XXXV

desert birds a way past all desolation

(Remixed poem from page 68)